POST OFFICES

Julian Stray

SHIRE PUBLICATIONS

Published in Great Britain in 2010 by Shire Publications Ltd,
Midland House, West Way, Botley, Oxford OX2 0PH,
United Kingdom.

44-02 23rd Street, Suite 219, Long Island City,
NY 11101, USA.

E-mail: shire@shirebooks.co.uk   www.shirebooks.co.uk

A CIP catalogue record for this book is available from the
British Library.

Shire Library no. 594 . ISBN-13: 978 0 74780 785 8

Julian Stray has asserted his right under the Copyright,
Designs and Patents Act, 1988, to be identified as the
author of this book.

Designed by Myriam Bell Design, France and typeset
in Perpetua and Gill Sans.
Printed in China through Worldprint Ltd.

10 11 12 13 14   10 9 8 7 6 5 4 3 2 1

COVER IMAGE
A postmaster serves a customer in his cramped post office
at Latimer, Buckinghamshire, 1947.

TITLE PAGE IMAGE
'White on black' post office sign, an early example of an
emerging brand.

CONTENTS PAGE IMAGE
A 1762 letter to James Gordon, an important wine dealer,
care of the Jamaica Coffee House, London. Coffee Houses
were one of the earliest places where letters could be left or
collected. A Foreign Office 'Bishop Mark' has been applied
on arrival in London: 'NO / 30' indicating '30 November'.
Bishop Marks were the first hand-struck postmarks in the
world, first introduced in 1661.

ACKNOWLEDGEMENTS
Thanks to Chris Taft, Rebecca Thomlinson, Alison Norris,
Vyki Sparkes, Barry Attoe and Martin Devereux for their
support and assistance. Special thanks to Deborah Turton
for her support, proofreading and editing.

The author and images for this book were provided by
The British Postal Museum & Archive.

All images are © Royal Mail Group Ltd 2010, courtesy
of The British Postal Museum & Archive,
www.postalheritage.org.uk; with the exception of
the following:

The British Postal Museum & Archive, pages 32, 34
(top and middle), 39 (top), 42 (top), 43, 44 (top),
45 (top), 46, 47 (top), 48, 49 (bottom), and 50 (top);
F. Goodall print, page 6, obtained by The British Postal
Museum & Archive through the V&A purchase fund;
Letchworth Museum and Art Gallery, North Hertfordshire
Museum Service, page 9; and Julian Stray pages
20 (bottom), 21 (bottom), 25, 27, 36 (right),
45 (bottom), 47 (bottom), 50 (bottom), and 51.

Shire Publications is supporting the Woodland Trust, the UK's leading woodland conservation charity, by funding the dedication of trees.

CONTENTS

EARLY POST OFFICES

POST OFFICES hold a special place in the hearts and minds of British people. They are frequently places of trust, and the postmaster or postmistress is often held in high regard within the local community. A post office may be one of the grandest buildings in a city, but most post offices are far humbler affairs – often single-counter offices managed by a sole shopkeeper, and of immense importance to the local population.

Today's post offices are broadly a mixture of main 'crown offices' and local 'sub-offices'. A crown office, in the centre of a town, provides a full range of counter services and is exclusively devoted to this. The bulk of Britain's local post offices are smaller sub-offices, typically providing other facilities at the same premises, and remaining open for longer hours. In urban areas sub-offices are often found in newsagents' shops. In more rural areas a sub-office is typically situated in the village shop. Post offices make up one of the largest retail networks in Europe, yet these businesses evolved from very humble beginnings.

Britain's postal service originated in the reign of Henry VIII. Henry commanded that Sir Brian Tuke, the first Master of the Posts, set up 'posts' – connected roads and towns – 'in al places most expedient'. The resulting 'post roads' were a small number of routes along which messengers carried letters of court. At the beginning of the seventeenth century there were only four post roads: the post to Scotland; the post to Ireland; the post to Plymouth; and the post to Dover (and onward to the Continent). Post-horses were provided for couriers at towns at regular intervals along post roads so that they could travel unhindered, changing horses without delay. The people who ran these staging posts were the earliest postmasters and they were permitted to rent out post-horses to other travellers so long as they could still provide passing royal couriers with any horses they might require. Because their position allowed postmasters to command additional income, by providing accommodation and sustenance, some postmasters actually paid for their appointment.

In 1635 Charles I issued a proclamation that allowed the public to use his 'royal mail' service. This marked the beginning of what would, following an

Opposite:
A Country Post Office (1837), an oil painting by Edward Villiers Rippingille depicting the excited gathering outside a post office following the arrival of the village post. A posting aperture is visible inserted into the window frame.

Act of Parliament in 1660 under Charles II, become the General Post Office, a branch of government headed by the Postmaster General. The early service was, however, limited. Almost all letters were sent via London, with no mechanism for transferring mail directly between post towns not on the same post road. Not until around 1696 was a series of 'cross posts' established linking these roads and improving the service. Letters were taken to 'letter-receiving houses', from which they were carried between post towns. Letters were charged for by distance travelled and the number of sheets included, or by weight for 'heavy' letters, making posting a letter an expensive proposition.

The earliest letter-receiving houses were at inns where the innkeeper accepted mail brought in for posting by the local community. These local representatives were known as 'deputies'. They needed to be trustworthy, as the *Post Office Instructions to Surveyors* of 10 November 1736 highlights:

> When you get to Petersfield you are to enquire into the Ability and Character of the Person who keeps the Old White Hart Inn there, and report to their Hon'rs whether you think him a proper Person to be Deputy at that Stage; enquire into the conduct of the present Deputy, & acquaint their Hon'rs whether he gives satisfaction to the Town of Petersfield and make a report thereof.

Post offices have always been a place at which news is exchanged, a focal point for gossip and the centre of a community. This F. Goodall print records the arrival of good news and bad.

The Post Office Stage Coach, an oil painting by Henry Alken Sr (1785–1851). Some coaching inns used by both mail coaches and stagecoaches (as here) also acted as post offices. Postmasters at these locations were referred to as 'deputies'.

The first local postal service was in London, established by a London merchant called William Dockwra. In 1680 Dockwra set up a penny post system, whereby letters were conveyed for a charge of only one penny – in flagrant defiance of the monopoly on letters held by the newly formed Post Office. He divided the area of his penny post into districts, each with a central sorting office, and established hundreds of 'letter-receiving offices', many in coffee houses. Post boys left and collected letters at the new 'penny post receiving houses'. In 1682 steps were taken by the Post Office to close the service. Subsequently, however, the Post Office re-established the same service as an official 'Post Office Penny Post', employing Dockwra as Controller from 1697.

In 1764 the Postmaster General obtained authority to establish in any city or town a penny post like that in London. The scheme was slow to get going but eventually letter-receiving houses began appearing in many towns. The first city outside London to have its own penny post was Dublin in 1773, followed by Edinburgh in 1773–4. As in London, this was initially a private venture but it became official in 1793, the same year that Manchester obtained its penny post.

Mail coaches were introduced in 1794, creating new routes that passed through many villages and towns previously distant from any postal facility. The times that local letter-receiving houses, increasingly referred to as 'post offices', were open were regulated by the town's clock, if it had one, while the time of despatch of mails was regulated by the mail-coach guards' timepieces (regulated to London time in England, Dublin

An eighteenth-century wooden sign once displayed outside an inn on a post road to indicate that the proprietor was licensed to rent post-horses to travellers.

time in Ireland). It was said that the time could be told accurately by the arrival and departure of the mails at the local post office.

By this time it was only in exceptional cases, and with the express permission of the Postmaster General, that a person who owned or managed a public house could be appointed to a Post Office position. Shopkeepers, tradesmen and even schoolmasters were employed as they were regarded as more reputable. Because debt was the most common cause of dismissal, each sub-postmaster was also required to provide two sureties to act as guarantors. A post office could be situated in an individual's shop or place of work, even his house. For example, when the mounted post boy arrived at Paignton, Devon, he passed the village's entire incoming post through a 12 by 10 inch window into the postmaster's sitting room.

Most postal transactions took place through a hatch or window into the post office. The public were required to stand outside, whatever the weather. Each postmaster was expected to furnish his office with the required fittings with which to transact official business. A press or drawer was provided to hold letters awaiting delivery or collection, and there was a separate drawer in which to keep official papers and instructions. A small door or movable pane of glass would be situated in a window at each office, through which the postmaster could 'attend to applications from the public'. Most offices were furnished with a hand-stamp to provide transit marks or for use on official forms.

The post office in Week Street, Maidstone, Kent, was typical. Between 1810 and 1841 George Hulbard, a hatter by trade, ran the office. Postal facilities were limited to a side of the shop window about 2 feet wide in which there was a small opening. Into this all letters had to be placed. If the public wished to make enquiries of the postmaster they had to walk up a narrow passage about 3 feet wide and knock on a little window at the end.

Apertures enabling the public to post letters were provided in the wall or window of post offices from at least the mid-eighteenth century. An instruction was issued to all Letter Receivers in London in 1814 that:

> Every Office, or Receiving House, must have a letter box in the Front for Unpaid Letters. It must be fixed in a part convenient for Public access; be large and strong, and kept locked, with the Key out, till the proper time of emptying for each dispatch. The words 'Unpaid Letter Box' to be painted on it.

Between 1846 and 1856 vertical apertures, then considered more secure from theft, were stipulated. If more than one despatch of letters was made, a second box was provided for 'too late' letters. Some post offices made do with a hatch through which senders could pass their letters.

Every post office is provided with hand-stamps for a variety of administrative purposes. This remarkable survivor is an 1837 wooden hand-stamp from Chislehurst post office, Kent, and was used to indicate that the 2d postage rate had been paid.

When the first official post office opened at Leamington Spa in 1833, a window was removed from the boot and shoe shop belonging to Mr Enoch, the newly appointed postmaster, and replaced with a small black door carrying a tiny knocker, which, when struck, secured the door's opening, enabling the public to hand in letters. Latterly, postmasters were instructed to display the words 'Post Office' in large letters on their house or business premises.

A local postmaster was paid a sum of money by the Post Office based on the amount of work transacted. This often caused dissatisfaction as it was felt that such remuneration was insufficient for the equipment supplied and work carried out. When Alexander Dingwall was appointed postmaster of Aberdeen in 1787, he was expected to supply not only the post office itself, but also clerks, coal, lighting, sealing wax, twine and any other equipment required by his employer. For this he was paid £89 15s *per annum*. Salaries were paid quarterly. Only persons above the age of sixteen could be employed by a postmaster and then only if they had made a declaration before a magistrate. This was because the theft of letters was a capital offence.

In 1774 the Court of the King's Bench decided that letters could be delivered free of (additional) charge within the limits of a post town. It was left for the Postmaster General to define the limits. Once letters had been brought to a town, they were sorted by the postmaster and sent out to the outlying streets by messenger. The messenger would summon residents to come and collect their letters by ringing a bell; ten or twelve letters was considered a large delivery.

Early postmasters were obliged to provide an aperture through which letters could be posted into their premises. This example, from the post office at Baldock, Hertfordshire, carries the signwriting from its use during the reign of William IV (1830-7). The back shows that it was reversed and reused when Victoria acceded to the throne (1837–1901).

Local postmasters were responsible for delivering all letters within the boundary set by the Post Office Surveyor, or for seeing that a messenger or letter-carrier completed the duty. They were not bound to take letters to persons beyond the free delivery area but could do so on mutual agreement of a fee for this service.

Up to 1794 post office receivers (or sub-postmasters) were paid at the rate of one penny for every ten letters they received at their office. From 1795 salaries were increased to £1 *per annum* for each letter-carrier employed at their office and an additional £1 *per annum* for each mailbag received from passing mail coaches.

There were few post offices in the eighteenth and early nineteenth centuries. Posting facilities were provided by 'bell men', who carried locked satchels with posting slots in the top and rang a hand-bell to alert the public to their whereabouts. Bell men were phased out following the introduction of post boxes in the mid-nineteenth century.

Old Post Office, Tintagel

Post offices were popular postcard subjects. This early card by Valentines shows the Old Post Office, Tintagel, Cornwall. The office was originally a fourteenth-century manor house. It became a letter-receiving house in 1844 when the village began to generate more than 120 letters a week. The post room moved in 1892 and the building is now owned by the National Trust.

The sub-post office at Shipton-under-Wychwood, Oxfordshire, c.1900. Opened before 1847, this office relinquished its title as England's oldest post office when it closed in March 1975.

By the end of the nineteenth century wages also included payments based on the number of stamps sold, and commission for other business such as postal orders, money orders and savings bank services. Salaries were revised every three years and the ratio of salary to commission was roughly 50:50.

Post offices quickly became the hub of a community. They became a place where people met to collect or drop off letters, or to engage in business discussion or idle gossip while waiting for the postmaster to resume his role. Writing of its local office in 1909, the *Dundee Advertiser* asserted: 'Since the morning of 23 May 1862, when it was opened, the Post Office has been the hub of Dundee … the convenient rendezvous for all parts of the City.'

A head postmaster would provide a notice to local sub-postmasters giving information, such as the contracted hours of attendance, to be placed in the office window. In the eighteenth and early nineteenth centuries, offices were usually required to open for business at 7.00 a.m. from 1 March to 31 October, and at 7.30 a.m. for the remainder of the year. On Sundays they normally closed by 10.00 a.m. provided they had been open for a full hour after the mail delivery began. On Sundays, all normal transactions could be carried out except the issue or payment of money orders. There was only one delivery on a Sunday.

Before the mid-nineteenth century postmasters were appointed by the Patronage Secretary of the

Of modest appearance, the post office at Bacup, Lancashire, was first occupied in 1865. Two apertures were provided for letters in one of the windows. The office had been vacated by February 1892.

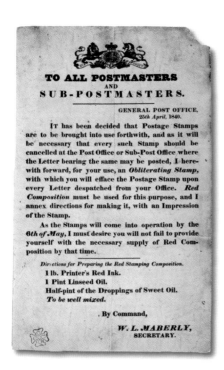

TO ALL POSTMASTERS
AND
SUB-POSTMASTERS.

GENERAL POST OFFICE,
25th April, 1840.

IT has been decided that Postage Stamps are to be brought into use forthwith, and as it will be necessary that every such Stamp should be cancelled at the Post Office or Sub-Post Office where the Letter bearing the same may be posted, I herewith forward, for your use, an *Obliterating Stamp,* with which you will efface the Postage Stamp upon every Letter despatched from your Office. *Red Composition* must be used for this purpose, and I annex directions for making it, with an Impression of the Stamp.

As the Stamps will come into operation by the *6th of May,* I must desire you will not fail to provide yourself with the necessary supply of Red Composition by that time.

Directions for Preparing the Red Stamping Composition.

1 lb. Printer's Red Ink.
1 Pint Linseed Oil.
Half-pint of the Droppings of Sweet Oil.
To be well mixed.

. By Command,

W. L. MABERLY,
SECRETARY.

The world's first postage stamp, the Penny Black, officially went on sale on 6 May 1840. Every post office received sheets of stamps, each containing 240 or £1's worth. These were imperforate, requiring postmasters to cut stamps from the sheet. Offices also received an 'obliterating handstamp', a Maltese cross, an impression of which is at the bottom of this notice.

Treasury on the advice of local members of Parliament. Such appointments were usually made to local shopkeepers who provided the necessary space in their premises in exchange for an allowance from the Post Office; local sub-postmasters also provided additional counter staff where the volume of business required this. In addition to sub-post offices, there still remained the network of letter-receiving houses where the public could simply hand in letters. The owners of small shops acting as receiving houses were paid a commission based on the number of letters handled by them.

There remained, however, large parts of the country where no post office existed. In addition, using the post was an expensive procedure, with the *recipient* paying not only for the number of sheets of paper but also for the distance the letter had travelled. A defining change occurred in 1840 when Rowland Hill introduced a uniform basic postage rate of 1d per half ounce, paid by the *sender*. This not only simplified administration but led to a huge increase in use of the postal system. The inhabitants of small villages and hamlets previously deprived of any post office began to use the relatively cheap postal service that now became available to them. By the 1850s there was an increasing demand and need for sub-post offices on a scale previously unthought of. This led to the opening of new post offices even in the remotest parts of Britain and Ireland. Such an increase is not surprising when one looks at the increase in mail volumes. From 67 million letters posted in 1839, this rose to 242 million following postal reform in 1840 and over a billion by 1875.

To accommodate the growing number of letters, free-standing 'pillar boxes', into which letters could be posted, were introduced across Britain following their trial in the Channel Islands in 1852. A Rural Post Revision was carried out from 1851 to 1859. Post Office surveyors visited every village and hamlet in the country to review postal arrangements. Many new post routes were established and new sub-post offices opened. Rural communities found themselves included in the nation's postal network for the first time. If a village did not warrant a post office, then posting facilities, in the form of wall boxes (introduced in 1857), were often placed there.

From 1854 the power to appoint postmasters altered. Where a postmastership was worth more than £175 *per annum*, the postmaster was appointed by the Postmaster General; if it was below this figure, the Treasury

Opened in 1829, the new General Post Office in St Martin's-le-Grand, London, provided a public counter, housed mail guards, an armoury, sorting and delivery staff and administration facilities, and was the residence of the Postmaster General. Designed by Sir Robert Smirke, the architect responsible for the frontage of the British Museum, the building was demolished in 1912–13, causing a public outcry.

retained the power of appointment. In 1854 there were over nine thousand country sub-post offices; by the end of the century this had risen to almost sixteen thousand, plus another five thousand or so town sub-post offices. The Post Office was one of only a handful of organisations that provided such national coverage in the nineteenth century. Public utilities were provided by local authorities as banks were frequently regional and even the grouping of the railways had yet to occur.

The public area at the London Chief Office, King Edward Building (built 1905–10), was 160 feet long and 60 feet wide. It featured Irish green and Italian white marble, with bronze fittings. The mahogany counter ran almost the entire length of the main hall.

Above: Aberdeen post office, 1907: an example of the Scottish Baronial style.

Above right: Post offices were for many years frequently among the largest and grandest of public buildings in a town. This photograph records the construction of Luton's new post office in May 1881.

The buildings in which post offices were housed subsequently altered dramatically. They became grander, exhibiting impressive architecture that made an office stand out on a high street. Shopkeepers increasingly became unable to provide the larger, bespoke facilities required and so the Post Office took on the responsibility of providing these grander premises at its own expense, employing local architects and builders to erect what would become known as 'crown post offices' in larger towns. When a post office was built and maintained by the government Office of Works, it was designated a Crown Office Class I. Where possible the Post Office would rent or lease a building. These offices were designated Crown Office Class II.

Another development was the issue of official notices to postmasters. Occasionally these were intended to inform counter staff of a change in work procedure but more frequently they were used to advertise new products, dates of posting, new weight limits or postage rates, and to ensure all offices provided a uniform service. Such posters were displayed in the post office counter area while notices detailing opening hours were positioned at the entrance. The standard official appearance of such notices and associated post office paraphernalia presented a familiar and professional face to the public. Official notices were, and frequently still are, supplemented by church, council and police notices. Post offices were increasingly regarded as trusted and safe places at which to transact business other than the simple sending and receipt of letters.

By the beginning of the twentieth century post offices had become a national as well as local institution. By 1900 there were 906 head post offices, 255 associated branch offices, 4,964 town sub-offices and 15,815 country post offices – a total of 21,940 post offices across the United Kingdom.

The opening of a new post office was often the cause for a celebration to which local dignitaries, including the mayor, were invited. Here crowds gather in the street at Glastonbury, Somerset, for the opening of their new post office in August 1938.

Dignitaries at the new post office counter at Glastonbury. Mrs J. Alexander, wife of the Deputy Mayor, sells the first stamps available from the counter to Mrs W. A. L. Hucker, the Mayoress.

The sub-postmistress, Miss MacGregor, stands outside Drymen Station post office. The long shadows indicate an early morning mail collection being made by the small Morris van.

THE POST OFFICE NETWORK

Today's POST OFFICE NETWORK stems from recommendations made by the Hobhouse Committee in 1908. This House of Commons committee recommended that sub-post offices earning £500 *per annum* in London, or £250 in the provinces, should be replaced by crown offices offering the full range of services. This practice was adopted by the Post Office and largely continued until the mid-twentieth century, with the £250 limit being raised to £350 between the two world wars. Postmasters running local sub-offices would be paid a wage and remunerated for the work carried out at their office, based on unit credits assigned to the various items of work.

When a change in status from sub-office to crown office was appropriate an official application was made to the Treasury. In 1906 there were thirty-two post offices receiving over £500 *per annum*, all but one of which were in London. By 1938 this figure had risen to 220. Following the introduction of various payments during the Second World War, however, the number of higher-earning offices increased dramatically to 2,600.

After the Second World War the Post Office considered for conversion to crown office status every sub-office in which a sub-postmaster received a gross salary of £800 per annum. There were complaints by some sub-postmasters who resented these proposals. They received some support in the national press, including the *Daily Mail* in 1949:

Opposite: Grimsby post office, 1910. The architect, J. Rutherford, along with Sir Edward Tanner and James Williams, was responsible for some of the most important post offices of the nineteenth and early twentieth centuries.

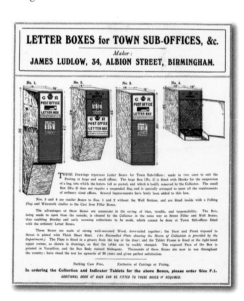

LETTER BOXES for TOWN SUB-OFFICES, &c.

Maker:

JAMES LUDLOW, 34, ALBION STREET, BIRMINGHAM.

Right: Sub-postmasters were originally required to provide posting facilities at their offices at their own expense. Many opted for cheap, locally made wooden boxes, known as 'carpenter's boxes'. Some manufacturers supplied ready-made boxes. The most prolific of these was James Ludlow, who took over the manufacture and supply of boxes from Edward Cole at his Birmingham workshop.

Sub-postmasters seem to be a tranquil race. They move from the sugar to the stamps, calm, unhurried, and apparently untouched by political blasts from without. But this picture is deceptive. The quiet world of sub-postmasters is rent with dissension ... he is more a slave to the clock than most of us. His day behind the post office counter is split into 18-second units, all timed by a stopwatch.

The early head post office at King's Lynn, Norfolk, was austere and redolent of Victorian empire. Its replacement (below), photographed in 1931, was built on the same footprint. Designed by D. N. Dyke of the Office of Works, it retained an official look with brick façade and large windows but was less forbidding to visitors.

Smaller post offices had begun to look a little tired, particularly when compared to more modern crown offices. Despite recognition that the financial position of sub-postmasters had considerably improved since 1908, postal facilities were often inadequate and even large sub-offices seldom matched the standard at crown offices. Complaints were made by the public but, in fairness, this decline was due to the growth in work outstripping capacity at post offices originally thought to be perfectly adequate. Small grant payments were occasionally provided by the Post Office to facilitate improvements, but sub-postmasters were usually quick to improve the situation themselves following official admonishment. Expectation was high: in addition to providing the required counter facilities for dealing with the public, sub-postmasters were also expected to provide requisite fittings for postmen operating out of their office. These included sorting frames for letters and parcels, and tables and chairs for the postmen.

Bigger post offices were built in larger towns and cities. Not only could the public use the entire range of services at these offices but they also acted as regional hubs from which the surrounding smaller post offices could be administered. Some post offices were complex communities in themselves with different grades of employee performing a range of services. When the new post office at Grimsby opened in April 1910, it combined both postal and telegraph facilities. This large and commodious office was indicative of the huge amount of mail traffic that passed through the port. This included foreign mail and large quantities of fish traffic — some 120,000 such parcels being collected in one year alone. The new office must have been as remarkable for its smell as for its design features.

In 1912 the Post Office took control of the great majority of the United Kingdom's telephones. It was now responsible for a number of buildings previously owned by the National Telephone Company. Some were retained, but mostly only those that could be used for both postal and telephone purposes. An extension of the building programme was required to support these. Between the First and Second World Wars there were three main types of office in addition to local sub-offices. These were:

Crown Office Class I: freehold or leasehold buildings, provided, equipped and maintained by the Office of Works (except light and heating).

Crown Office Class II: buildings taken on lease, fitted up and maintained by Post Office funds without intervention from the Office of Works. Such offices would normally have been the smaller head post offices, and salaried sub-post offices.

Allowance Office: provided by the Post Office under an allowance of rent. Fittings were provided by the Post Office though in some cases the landlord provided these with the cost covered in the rent paid to the landlord.

Allowance post offices were a diminishing class to which additions were made only in exceptional circumstances.

The division of power between the Office of Works (subsequently the Ministry of Works), responsible for freehold post offices, and the Post Office, responsible for leasehold offices, soured relations between the departments. The Ministry of Works was not in the business of expending more on a functional building than was strictly necessary, preferring more austere offices. Herbert Samuel, a man who twice served as Postmaster General (1910–14 and 1915–16), was dissatisfied with this and stated his belief that:

> The State has the duty of erecting its public buildings in a manner which
> will contribute to the dignity and the beauty of the towns in which they are
> situated, and particularly is this the case when those buildings are for the
> purpose of conducting a vast and very profitable business, and are daily
> entered by great numbers of people.

Many smaller post offices were refurbished during the inter-war years. Light-coloured panels and steel-framed glazing helped provide brighter facilities for a public experiencing momentous change in the national economy. The 1933 update at Walton post office, Liverpool, is a striking example.

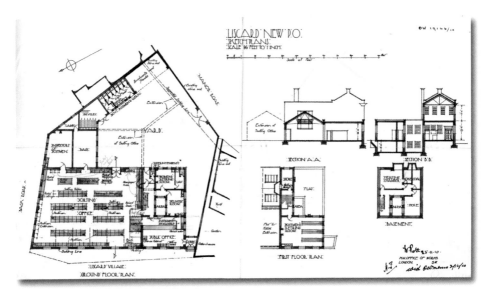

Above: The 1910 Office of Works plan for Liscard post office, Wirral, reveals the extent of the building beyond the public area. It combines a sorting and delivery office with residential quarters.

Construction of post offices did not stop during the First World War. The Post Office was unusual in that large impressive buildings continued to be built because the requirement for effective communication was more important than ever. This has left an important architectural legacy from a period otherwise poorly represented.

If a town was situated in the centre of a postal district or attracted a large amount of trade, a port for example, a head post office would be built to a more impressive design. Such offices included Birmingham, Bristol, Glasgow, Liverpool and Manchester. Smaller branch offices were also updated where possible.

The 1920s and 1930s were the golden age of bespoke post office buildings, produced by the Ministry of Works. The Ministry's architects' division had a self-contained Post Office Section and almost two thousand Class I offices were built up to 1931. There was also an increased requirement for post offices that could also act as specialised telephone exchanges. This combination of functions dictated a move away from Class II offices towards an increasing number of Class I offices.

The Post Office acted as client, with the Ministry as its architect. Architects such as Bulloch, Dyke, Llewellyn, Rees and Seccombe began to produce traditional designs for the Post Office that abandoned classicism in

Left: A keystone at Hastings crown post office, Sussex. Hermes, the messenger to the gods, frequently appears above entrances to post offices built in the inter-war years.

Aldershot post office, Hampshire, incorporated many design features introduced by the Ministry of Works that helped to create a generic appearance. Customers using the small but functional area at Aldershot were separated from counter clerks by a wire screen.

favour of the neo-Georgian and neo-Tudor styles. Local influence sometimes led to buildings that contrasted with the more formal Class I offices – utilising local building materials, tradition and style. More frequently, the post offices of this period featured doorcases with fanlights, sash windows and hipped, tile-hung roofs. Brick largely replaced stone frontages and a remarkable symmetry was proffered. Roman lettering on signs offered a 'house style' – a forerunner of what would later become 'retail branding'. These are among the most distinctive post offices ever built. The architectural intent was well expressed by Lord Gerald Wellesley, Fellow of the Royal Institute of British Architects:

Many larger and older post offices are now deemed unfit for their original purpose. Despite no longer acting as a working post office, the former head office in Leeds remains a focal point for the city.

A Post Office must be in a prominent position. It should look dignified and permanent, and should, as far as possible, harmonize with its surroundings … the public office, which should, of course, be of a size adequate to the number frequenting it, should, in the larger instances, have doors giving on to the streets at both ends … must be very well lit, and this may mean windows on the ground floor which ideally speaking, are disproportionately large compared with those in the upstairs offices. A clock and prominently displayed letter-box are also features of a Post Office front.

The interior work in late-nineteenth-century Ministry of Works buildings was frequently undertaken by local tradesmen. Many offices combined a public main office in front with a sorting and delivery office behind. A telegraph

Above: Falmouth post office illustrated on the 1951 poster by Maurice Rickards advertising the *Post Office Review* of Post Office activities.

Right: The branch post office at Old Street, London, was designed by J. Emberton and opened in 1958. Six posting apertures were included in the frontage for various classes of local, country and overseas mail.

instrument room might also be included. Upper floors provided space for offices, stores or occasionally accommodation for senior staff or a caretaker. However, as the need for departmental space increased, any top-floor resident would be instructed to find alternative accommodation; occasionally an allowance would be paid to cover the extra cost. Some offices also incorporated an inspection chamber to enable covert surveillance of staff to be made if there was cause for suspicion of malpractice or even theft.

By the 1950s the Ministry of Works was responsible for over five thousand post office buildings. Many older offices had become unsuitable for purpose, being either in a bad state of repair or simply too small. By contrast, the neo-Georgian post offices of the early to mid-twentieth century frequently lent themselves to expansion and alteration in the decades that followed. In the late 1950s and early 1960s post office frontages were revamped. This led to an increasingly standardised frontage for post offices.

During the mid-twentieth century the Post Office was spending £10 million annually on new buildings. A joint Post Office and Ministry of Works Research and Development Group was formed to look into the

The public area at Old Street post office served a mixture of city businesses and local residents. A more modern appearance, similar to a bank's, had begun to be adopted.

possibility of reducing the cost of individual post office buildings. The first building planned by the group was an automatic telephone exchange at Altrincham, Cheshire, erected in 1960. The second project was a new £64,000 minimalist head post office at Hitchin, Hertfordshire. The whole office, opened in February 1962, was built for two-thirds the cost of a traditional office.

Public service counters were also redesigned to become 'all-purpose', and a new plate-glass screen design was adopted for most subsequent new or reconstructed offices. New features introduced at Hitchin post office included 'Service here' lights that could be switched to 'Closing' when a clerk was about to go off duty. In keeping with modern ideas at the time, ballpoint pens were supplied for the public to use. Self-service suites were

Hitchin post office in Hertfordshire, photographed soon after opening in 1962, was built to a modular design that excluded extraneous detail but offered capacity for expansion. It cost 60 per cent less to construct than comparable offices and was regarded as the model for all subsequent post offices.

Hitchin post office interior, 1963, shows the lowered ceilings and open-plan appearance that were incorporated into subsequent post office designs.

also installed, one inside and one outside. The exterior suite sold stamps, stamped stationery and three denominations of postal order, and incorporated a change machine. It was felt that such facilities would reduce the number of customers who needed to enter the office. In the late 1960s, in a bid to deal with rising costs, to improve staff recruitment, and as a partial response to complaints, revised hours of business were introduced at crown offices. These were now open from 9 a.m. to 5.30 p.m. (4.30 p.m. on Saturdays). Offices in some larger towns were open even longer.

The adoption of a 'modular' design, while not necessarily an identifiable brand, meant that post offices could be built to meet the requirements of any part of the country. The 1965 post office at Kingswood, Bristol, was built at a cost of just over £55,000 and was part of what the Post Office called 'a scheme to provide

Left: After 1969, when the Post Office became a public corporation and its relationship with the Ministry of Works ended, local architects designed new offices. Guildford's North Street post office (1970–2), by architects Roman Halter and Associates, was a radical departure from previous offices; the building incorporated wrap-around glazing and a projecting gazebo.

post offices which give pleasant surroundings in which the public can do their business'.

In 1969 the Post Office became a public corporation, and the Ministry of Works ceased designing post offices. Its successor, the Property Services Agency, took control of all buildings for government departments. This was also the end of any form of generic house style for post offices. Instead, teams of architects were commissioned as required when new buildings were proposed. Contractors were now given more opportunity to express their own flair in building layouts and materials. One of the first of the resulting new generation of buildings was Guildford's North Street post office.

Where a post office was situated within a general store that offered a wide range of other products, the availability of post office counter services was usually proclaimed proudly and boldly on the exterior of the building. Not only did such branding draw in additional customers, but it became an official requirement at each office. Some sub-postmasters continue to follow the old requirement of including the town name on their post office frontage; others simply combine 'post office' with their primary source of income as in 'post office and stores'.

Above:
A two-counter position post office operates at the rear of the information centre in Ambleside, Cumbria. A large-capacity 'C' type pillar box is testament to the combined volume of local and tourist mail at this popular Lake District town.

Left:
Sub-postmistress Jackie Walker runs the post office at Baston, Lincolnshire, while her husband, Jonathon, manages the combined village stores.

25

A major administrative change occurred in 1986, when the Post Office was reorganised into three separate businesses – Royal Mail Letters, Royal Mail Parcels and Post Office Counters. The following year Post Office Counters Limited became a wholly-owned subsidiary of the Post Office.

By the mid-1980s an average of 27 million customers each week were visiting the 22,398 post offices in the United Kingdom. 1,566 of these post offices were crown offices; the remainder were 20,832 'scale-payment sub-offices', each owned and managed within the private sector on an agency basis.

The majority of modern local post offices are scale-payment sub-offices, operated by a sub-postmaster supplementing a business income with earnings derived from the postal business also transacted at his office. Some offices provide additional facilities for one or more delivery staff; this can be more efficient than having postmen travelling large distances out of major towns to deliver in more remote areas. In the twenty-first century, Royal Mail employs the delivery staff, though the postmaster is still responsible for the provision of facilities and much of their day-to-day management.

The Post Office traditionally makes no financial contribution to the fitting out of local sub-post offices. A sub-postmaster is not only required to fit out a post office counter at his own expense but is also responsible for the purchase of the sign that hangs outside, regardless of office size or status. Some signs are illuminated; others have been designed to blend more

The post office at Castlebay on the isle of Barra in the 1980s. In parts of the Highlands and islands of Scotland post office branches also display the Gaelic phrase for 'post office', *oifis à phuist*.

Post office at Borough Green, Kent. A rare surviving example of a Post Office Direction sign (POD), on a large 'A' type pillar-box, points to the nearest post office, in this case just a few feet away! Such signs have now frequently disappeared or been vandalised.

sympathetically into conservation areas, while a minority can be removed and installed on a temporary basis if an office is part-time. A sub-postmaster may retain the general colour scheme of his shop throughout, including that part from which he offers post office services. Other postmasters choose to adopt the colour specifications used in crown offices.

Some post offices have been in the same family for decades, being handed on to each new generation in turn. Often the post office is run as much for the sake of tradition and social duty as it is for the money that it generates. The role of sub-postmaster may also suit young parents, enabling them to commit time both to a business and to looking after growing children.

Traditionally, most towns had a crown or branch post office in or near their high street. A large number of these have now been converted to sub-office status. These post offices are most often visited in lunch breaks. In towns the local community is very different to that of a rural area: visitors are a mixture of nearby residents and local business employees. Here, efficiency and range of services are far more important than a wish for general conversation. Such offices are unlikely to carry on any other form of retail activity but concentrate instead on Post Office products and services. Many of these offices provide dedicated counters offering *bureau de change* facilities. If there are many businesses in the immediate area there may well be a dedicated counter for Special Delivery mail. The 1,500 main offices that existed in 1988 were reduced to six hundred over the following eighteen years. In 2000 about a thousand sub-post offices were in shops run by multiple convenience store chains, including Spar, Alldays, Forbuoys, Star News and Dillons. The network of post offices in the United Kingdom remained enormous.

SAVINGS BANK.

COUNTER SERVICES

ALMOST from the moment post offices began, the range of services available from them has been proudly promoted by notices, posters and signs, inside and out – all highlighting the vital importance of the post office to everyday life. Indeed, the post office and the services it provided were often viewed as instrumental to a town's growth.

In Leicester in the 1930s it was reported that:

> Modern civilisation and business could not have existed without the post office ... they embrace, a large portion of the lighter parcels traffic, telegraph and telephone work, savings bank business, insurance and annuity work, postal orders, licences, payment of old-age and widows' pensions, sale of Health and Unemployment Insurance stamps, National Savings Certificates, entertainment stamps, and a vast number of forms for practically every other Government department.

After mail collection and delivery – and before even the purchase of stamps became commonplace – the earliest services provided by post offices were financial. One of the first of these was the 'money order' service. Following its establishment by a private company in 1792, the money order service was taken on by the Post Office in 1838. A money order was an order for payment of a specified amount of money. Tradesmen favoured this method for its extra security: because the order was prepaid, it could not bounce. By 1871, however, the money order system had become expensive to operate and a replacement was suggested in the form of what would become known as a 'postal order' service.

Postal orders initially met with fierce resistance from Parliament. It was thought that the Post Office was attempting to introduce a new form of currency. Following slight amendments, however, the first postal orders went on sale on 1 January 1881. They could be bought or redeemed at any post office and soon became hugely popular. In the first three months of sale, £292,500 was transmitted via 646,989 postal orders.

Opposite:
Post office saving acted as a stepping stone for many new savers, moving them from piggy bank to bank account. Millions visited their post office every week to make deposits or withdrawals.

Postal orders were also very adaptable. In 1914, following the outbreak of the First World War, the government withdrew gold from circulation and, despite earlier assurances, on 7 August 1914 declared postal orders 'for the time being to be currency to be used and accepted for all purchases for which gold and silver coins are used'. Postal orders were issued for this purpose without counterfoil and free of all additional payments at post offices. Their use as currency continued until 4 February 1915. After the war their general usage fell because of the economic depression and it was not until the 1930s that numbers again increased. In 1936–7 343,900,000 postal orders, with a combined value of £88,900,000, changed hands. They were again permitted as legal tender for a brief period at the start of the Second World War, in an attempt to stop the hoarding of coin.

Postal orders were also adopted for the payment of old-age pensions when these were introduced on 1 January 1909. From this date, 596,038 people were eligible to visit one of 23,500 local post offices to collect their pension. Pension books consisted of twenty-five postal orders – enough for six months. Such service provision, like the later introduction of the family allowance, made post offices increasingly central to daily life.

Above: A Norman Howard poster advertising *The Post Office Guide*, 1937. The Guide was published between 1856 and 1986 and contained a wealth of information on Post Office services.

Right: By the late 1920s, post office frontages were heavy with advertising. This branch office at Southampton Row, Bloomsbury, London, displays a variety of notices relating to overseas mail and telephone services.

A one-shilling deposit slip for the Post Office Savings Bank, completed with twelve one-penny postage stamps. Children were encouraged to save using these forms.

Postal orders have long remained a favourite with the public; in addition to acting as a reasonably secure method of payment for small amounts, they were very popular as a gift to be enclosed in birthday and Christmas cards. Doting uncles and aunts possibly hoped that favoured nephews and nieces would deposit the money in a savings account when forced to visit their local post office to cash each order. Despite usage gradually tailing off, there was a resurgence towards the end of the twentieth century with the onset of online auction sales; postal orders were an ideal method of making small, secure payments by post.

Another popular post office institution, the Post Office Savings Bank, began in 1861 to provide savings facilities for ordinary people. Huge numbers made regular visits to their local post office to deposit savings because banks were mostly situated only in larger towns and cities. From an initial seven hundred post offices offering the facility, the figure rose to 2,500 branches within two years. It became a favoured method of saving for friendly societies, provident institutions and thousands of individuals who saved up their pennies in home savings banks. By 1901 there were over 8.5 million accounts with deposits totalling over £140 million. By 1967 the overall savings balance stood at £1,731 million. Such has been

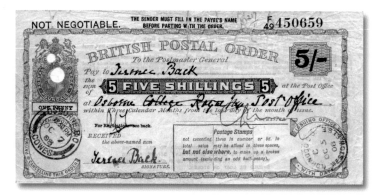

In 1910 George Archer-Shee, a young naval cadet, was accused of having stolen and cashed a 5-shilling postal order belonging to a fellow cadet, Terence Back. The case became a cause célèbre, inspiring Terence Rattigan's play *The Winslow Boy*.

The Post Office Savings Bank was created in 1861 to restore the confidence of savers following the collapse of many private schemes. Millions of people opened accounts, though savings books often lay forgotten in drawers. Some 250 books are returned each week to be converted into decimal currency. Books have now been replaced with cards.

the popularity of saving through the post office that post offices continued to act as agents when, on 1 October 1969, the Post Office ceased to be a government department and gave up control of what was then called the National Savings Bank.

One reason why everyone at some point visits the post office counter is to purchase postage stamps. From the introduction of the Penny Black stamp in 1840 as part of Rowland Hill's scheme for universal penny postage, stamps have been associated with post offices. By the twentieth century stamps were being purchased not only for postage purposes, but also as collectable 'philatelic' items, particularly on their first day of issue. Such was the frequency of counter visits solely for stamps that vending machines were developed enabling the purchase of stamps from post offices without the inconvenience of queuing.

The issuing of licences has also long been a function of post offices. Licences for dogs, guns, wireless and television and vehicle driving licences have all been processed and sold through post offices. Radio (or wireless) licences were available between November 1922 and February 1971. The first television licence, issued in June 1946, cost just £2.

A new banking service, National Giro, later renamed National Girobank, began in October 1968. The basic services were transfers between accounts, deposits into the account, and payments in the form of withdrawals or by Post Office 'cheque' to a third party. There were no facilities for overdrafts and no interest was paid. Market research had indicated a heavy demand for the service, and a computer system and accompanying administration had been set up to deal with one million accounts by the end of the first year. However, initial response was disappointing and by September 1967 only 150,000 accounts had been set up and the service was making a loss of £6 million a year. Marketing and publicity were improved, resulting in an upsurge in public interest. Four years later, however, the service was still struggling. New opportunities were explored and local authorities began to use Giro's cash deposit service to allow tenants to pay their rents. This also reduced the danger of attacks on rent collectors. Giro finally made a profit in 1974–5.

Phyllis Stone buys a stamp at an 'out of hours' machine at Oxford post office in 1936. These are type 'B' halfpenny and one-penny machines. In the 1920s and 1930s many stamp-vending machines were installed in the walls of post offices and attached to pillar boxes.

Eden Post Office, Northern Ireland, 1938. The sub-postmistress looks justly proud of her position in the community.

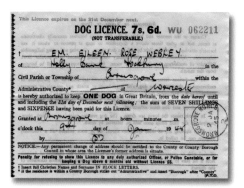

Above: Dog licences went on sale in 1869 and continued to be available at post offices until they were abolished in Great Britain (but not in Northern Ireland) in 1987.

Above: The first television licence revenue stamps, available from 1972, showed the actual value of the licence. From 1977, the letters 'M' (Monochrome) or 'C' (Colour) were incorporated in the design.

Right: Parcel weighing at Hildenborough post office, Kent, in 1935.

Another form of Post Office saving product, Premium Bonds, was introduced in 1956. Premium Bonds were introduced by the government to reduce inflation and encourage thrift among those more interested in winning prizes than earning interest. By the end of the first day of sale, 1 November 1956, £5 million worth had been sold. Winners were selected by ERNIE (Electronic Random Number Indicator Equipment), a machine that generated random numbers. By 1967, holdings of Premium Savings Bonds stood at over £586 million and 671,852 prizes totalling above £24 million were distributed that year. Though no longer responsible for Premium Bond sales, post offices remain a focal point for similar initiatives; post offices became the largest retailer of tickets for the National Lottery following its introduction in 1994.

The provision of a growing and varied range of services has required post office staff to adapt to meet public demand and service need. The introduction of a new inland Parcels Post service in 1883 (later renamed Parcel Post) caused practical problems for the Post Office and its employees. Every post office in the United Kingdom had to be equipped to deal with parcels. Every post office counter was supplied with parcel scales, and each office was supplied with new cork hand-stamps for stamping parcels. Offices were supplied with special handcarts, and delivery routes were altered so

that no member of staff was required to carry too heavy a load. The introduction of the Parcels Post brought another important change for staff: because letter carriers no longer carried only letters, they were renamed 'postmen'.

In smaller local post offices throughout the twentieth century a very small team of staff handled the work — sometimes just a single clerk. Larger offices with multiple counters occasionally dedicated one of these to a specific type of business such as Post Office Savings. Crown post offices usually handled work on a team basis, with a number of counter clerks transacting a range of services. This required a flexible work ethic. Regardless of the primary service at any one counter, each position would be fitted with a set of scales and carry a number of stamps (savings and postage) to meet general public demand. Some crown post offices would also have an enquiry position or, exceptionally, an enquiry office.

Post offices enabled communication by post and, latterly, by telecommunication. The telegraph service in the United Kingdom developed in conjunction with the spread of the railways in the 1840s and 1850s.

Following the arrival of pocket money in the shape of postal orders, Saturdays were the busiest day at the Duke of York's Royal Military School post office, Dover, in 1938. Sub-postmaster Regimental Quartermaster Sergeant W. G. Prescott MC provided postal, telegraph, savings bank and tuck-shop services for four hundred cadets.

A busy day at the post office counter. This scene has been repeated at countless post offices over the decades.

Right: A George Bass poster produced to promote the telegram service at crown and sub-post offices in 1950.

Far right: In 1925 Post Office engineers produced designs for a 'twenty-four hour post office'. Based on the 'K2' telephone kiosk designed by Giles Gilbert Scott, a 'stretched' variant, the 'K4', was introduced that included a post-box and two stamp-vending machines. Only fifty were manufactured and just a small number survive today.

In February 1870 the state formally took control of inland telegraphs from the various private companies, and on the same day the Post Office opened a public service from 2,800 telegraph offices. Initially, the majority of these were situated at railway stations but eventually the service was made available from post offices. A uniform minimum charge of one shilling for each inland message was introduced and 9,472,000 personal messages were sent in the first year, plus a further 700,000 press messages. However, by the mid-1930s, probably as a result of devastating news being sent during the First World War, the public associated telegrams with bad news. On the introduction of the sixpenny telegram a census was taken and this revealed that only 1 or 2 per cent of telegrams carried bad news. Some two-thirds of telegrams consisted of business messages and the remainder were of a social nature.

With telegrams came a new grade of post office worker, the 'telegraph messenger' (altered in 1908 to 'boy messenger'). Their duties consisted of delivering telegrams and taking replies back to the post office, plus some other minor tasks. In 1877 they were expected to work ten hours a day six days a week. While a wage scale existed, higher in towns than in the suburbs, many postmasters paid their boys by the number of messages or journeys made. Some post offices, usually rural ones, generated insufficient work to employ a dedicated boy messenger, and at these postmen were employed to deliver telegrams in addition to their normal duties. The 'boy messenger' grade was abolished in 1947 when a new grade of 'young postman' was created to carry out both telegram delivery and postal duties.

Left: During the Second World War mobile, tented post offices were produced for quick deployment to areas that had lost their office as a result of enemy bombing.

Below: A self-service kiosk providing postal products for drivers was trialled at Luton in 1964. Similar kiosks were planned for new motorway services. Although they were appreciated by the public, the costs proved prohibitive.

In 1896 the Post Office took over the National Telephone Company's trunk telephone service and in 1912 it became almost a monopoly within the United Kingdom. Post offices added telephone services to their list of facilities provided. As a result, a number of designs for telephone kiosks were introduced by the Post Office. Initially, kiosks were not normally installed at

In July 1982 Brush Railcoach 633 became the world's first post office tram. Passengers could buy postcards and stamps at the counter. Any mail posted received a special cachet. It ran in Blackpool until May 1985.

In the 1930s training schools for counter staff were established in London, Belfast, Birmingham, Bristol, Glasgow, Leeds, Liverpool and Manchester.

post offices unless likely to be remunerative. This altered as part of the 1935 Jubilee celebrations when the Postmaster General instructed that, where there was not already a call office, a kiosk should be installed at every village post office on the mainland of Great Britain and Northern Ireland, regardless of probable revenue.

Right: Post office services advertised on a 1980s 'menu' board, which would be fixed to a wall outside the office.

Below: A 1964 poster advertising Recorded Delivery for mail, produced for use on post office counter screens and on the sides of postal vans.

It is still possible to identify former post offices, long closed, by the external presence of either a post box or a telephone kiosk, sometimes both. As a result of its provision of postal and telephone services, the Post Office played an important part in the First World War by maintaining both communications and morale. Ration books were also distributed by post offices.

Throughout the twentieth century, most post offices, apart from the very smallest, dealt in postal, telegraph and telephone services in addition to providing a range of savings and other business related to other government departments and local authorities. As the number of services offered by post offices increased, so did the need for training for counter staff. However, provision often varied between town and country. Special courses would be run for counter clerks at Class I and II offices but there was little more than cursory instruction at rural sub-offices. Kathleen Roberts, a sub-postmistress at Bringsty Common in Herefordshire from 1955 to 1984, recalled: 'I used to come up seven days [a week] and help Granny Roberts, help her out in the post office, an' then I gradually took over, but I didn't have no training.'

By the early 1980s, the variety of services available at the local post office had barely changed from 1908, when the modern post office emerged following the recommendations of the Hobhouse Committee. Of the 150 different types of transaction available, ten accounted for 75 per cent of the workload. The top three of these were benefit payments (41 per cent), mails (17 per cent) and Girobank (16 per cent). By 1999 the Post Office had become the largest retailer in the United Kingdom, with more outlets than the major banks and building societies combined.

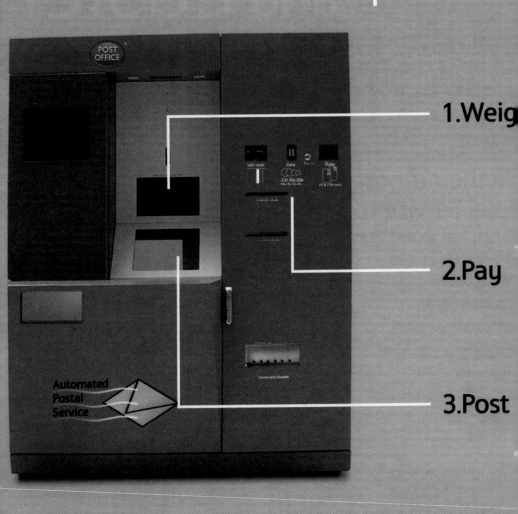

A new
way to post your
letters and parcels

POST OFFICE

1.Weig

2.Pay

3.Post

Automated Postal Service

in three easy steps

MODERN POST OFFICES

THE CROWN and sub-post office network that emerged during the twentieth century was an effective method of providing a variety of services to the public. By the end of the century, however, social and economic changes across Britain meant that this network was becoming increasingly difficult and costly to maintain.

Sub-postmasters were faced with ever-increasing overheads as rent, wages, rates and utility costs continued to spiral. The Post Office had become the United Kingdom's largest retailer, but annual losses stood at £50 million, despite a steady stream of customers carrying out 2,200 million transactions per year.

In a bid to increase profits at larger offices, in the early 1980s twenty-two post offices in the South-West trialled in-store video systems advertising post office counter services. Additional facilities also appeared, including photocopiers, advertising units and photo booths. By 1991 over five hundred photo booths had been installed in post offices, making them the largest provider in the country. A number of larger post offices were refurbished and new buildings reflected the latest image. Special uniforms for counter staff were trialled in Bristol and Torquay before being rolled out nationwide.

'Post Shops', a new type of retail outlet in post offices, were introduced in 1984. The first of these opened at Ashford in Kent. They offered packaging material (PostPak), stationery, greetings cards, BBC books, coin sets, philatelic products and, for younger customers, items based on the children's television character Postman Pat. In their first year of operation the original nineteen outlets generated a combined turnover of more than £1 million. This led to their increase and from 1997 Post Shops began selling gift vouchers for Marks & Spencer; 1,148 post offices were already stocking gift vouchers for other retailers including Boots and W. H. Smith.

With such a range of non-traditional services now being offered, a complaint often voiced by the public was the time it took to be served. An attempt to combat waiting time was made in the late 1970s by introducing a single-queue system. The Post Office also attempted to reduce waiting time

Opposite:
Leaflet explaining the 'Automated Postal Service' machine trialled in three post offices during 2004. 'With user-friendly touch-screen control and full, easy-to-follow instructions, using the Automated Postal Service is a breeze – just weigh, pay and away you go!'

Above: Sunayana Patel, counter clerk at Debden post office, Essex.

by commencing a series of training initiatives aimed at ensuring 97 per cent of customers were served within five minutes. Subsequently the Post Office Users' National Council stated that customers were being served more quickly than in supermarkets, banks or building societies; though there remained many who disputed that statement.

The Post Office believed that computerisation would ensure a viable future for the network. During 1982–3 trials were held at four post offices (Northampton, Plymouth, York and Portsmouth) of equipment (from four manufacturers) to automate counter services. Four sub-post offices joined the trial in 1983–4. The video display units and clerk-operated keyboards were linked to backroom computer processors that recorded and stored information. Three years later the government approved the investment in automation of 250 post offices in the Thames valley. This was a key development in the future of post office counters.

Transactions for Girobank, the Driver and Vehicle Licensing Agency and National Savings were all now automated. Further trials occurred in 1988 when electronic cash registers were installed at counters in eight post offices – four in London, three in Bournemouth and one in Chesterfield. This removed the chore of daily till balancing since the computers produced weekly accounts and enabled each post office to control product stock levels automatically.

Left: In the early 1990s ECCO+ terminals were installed in 650 main post offices throughout the United Kingdom. This increased the use of technology, streamlined accounting and sales, captured each transaction electronically, and reduced waiting time.

Trials continued with the installation at six Southampton post offices of electronic terminals permitting payment by debit cards, and the use of terminals at 120 post offices in Northern Ireland to capture transaction details electronically from customers using electricity power cards.

These developments led to the largest nationwide automation programme for post offices. In May 1996 ICL Pathway won the contract to provide swipe-card facilities in all of the United Kingdom's post offices. This was a massive undertaking, one of the largest IT projects in Europe. The project aim was to provide facilities for over 28 million claimants to receive one or more of twenty different Department of Social Security benefits and to prevent some £150 million fraudulent claims. With this project, the Post Office computerised network became twice as large as Britain's entire existing banking infrastructure. Despite initial success, the project foundered and Fujitsu, the new owners of ICL, were awarded a new contract to computerise all of the United Kingdom's post offices.

The subsequent £1 billion Horizon system expanded on the original Pathway system to provide the largest secure non-military Integrated Services Digital Network in Europe. It enabled post offices to make benefit payments more efficient and secure, and permitted other transactions such as the payment of gas, electricity and telephone bills, council tax and membership subscriptions electronically. There was also the ability to recharge smartcards and an increasing host of other services. This was how the Post Office envisaged a sustainable future – local post offices fitted with touch-screen termini, barcode readers, PIN pads, keyboards and printers issuing receipts.

By July 2000 8,365 post offices in Britain (over 40 per cent of the total number) had been fitted with the Horizon system. By February 2001 15,516 outlets were equipped. Soon plans were implemented to expand the system to allow locally printed postage labels as a partial replacement for stamps. Horizon is now installed in every post office in the United Kingdom.

Gillian Monrose, counter clerk at Diss crown post office, Norfolk, a traditional, old-style post office.

Sue Buckley, sub-postmistress at Bringsty Common scale-payment delivery office, Herefordshire, in 2007.

Alistair Meadows, sub-postmaster at Criccieth, Gwynedd, manages the mobile post office for the surrounding villages.

Community post offices have appeared in many locations. In 1991 Peter Redwood was running a community post office from his garden shed in Askerswell, Dorset.

Technology has enabled post offices to move into the twenty-first century. Conversely, it has also been one of the prime threats to their existence. By 2000 over 30 per cent of child benefit recipients, who would have traditionally claimed this at their local post office, had opted to have it paid directly into their bank accounts by automatic credit transfer. The knock-on effect for small and large post offices alike was obvious. If the public did not visit a post office to draw their money, then postmasters lost both those transactions and associated shop purchases.

For much of the older population, a weekly trip to the post office to collect a pension had previously been an outing to be savoured. It might be the only social interaction a person experienced from week to week. But as they became more technologically aware, even pensioners began to desert the post office, also opting for electronic payments. By 1992 between 30 and 40 per cent of new pensions were paid electronically; by the end of the century 50 per cent. As a result some smaller post offices began to close because they were no longer financially viable.

Notwithstanding technological advances, other solutions were required to maintain the post office network. Following early signs that rural post offices were becoming unviable, attempts were made during the 1980s to reverse this by employing staff on a part-time basis. This often helped maintain a service in quiet villages where a full-time office could not be justified. By 1988, more than forty village post offices that had shut because full-time opening was not viable had reopened as a result of the new part-time arrangements. Many offices also now operated as 'community post offices' – located in people's homes, in village or church halls, or in public houses. By the end of the 1980s there were 1,144 community offices, each opening for up to twenty hours a week.

A community post office might also offer a book exchange service, gardening products, and office facilities such a photocopying or Internet access. Post offices such as these could attract grants to

The White Lion pub at Selling, Kent, hosts a post office for just two hours a week. It is the only such service in the area.

help support the infrastructure, but it was the community that made them a success. Despite this new trend, rural post offices have continued to close when no one can be found to run them.

Further measures have led to the introduction of new twenty-first-century post office entities – approaches not very different from the original post offices. The first of these is the Mobile Service. Similar to the mobile post offices first used in the 1930s to provide postal facilities at events such as county shows and race meetings, the modern equivalent instead visits communities that have lost their own post office. Each van is fitted with an online Horizon system similar to larger permanent offices and provides similar services, albeit for only a few hours a week. Having arrived at each scheduled location, the van driver becomes the counter clerk. While many customers perceive this as a second choice, the service is better than none at all.

Some retail businesses have developed a post office 'Partner Service'. These offices are supported by, but independent of, a core sub-postmaster. Hours of business are the same as the opening hours of the host retailer and online

 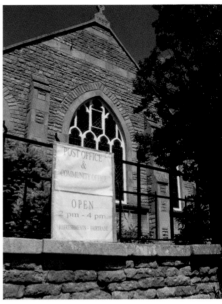

Above:
Sub-postmistress
Adele Stainsby
at an outreach
post office in a
Methodist chapel
in Rutland.

Above right:
Many outreach
post offices are
provided almost
exclusively for
local communities
and display only
low-key advertising
when open. The
post office at this
Methodist chapel
in Rutland opens
on Monday
afternoons, when
a fair-trade stall
also operates.

Horizon systems provide the typical range of post office services and products. As a result, post offices have appeared even in public houses. In 2004 Shepherd Neame, the Kent brewers, agreed to provide post office counter facilities at four public houses in rural villages on the North Downs near Faversham. The sub-postmistress of nearby Challock post office and grocery store carried a 'post office in a suitcase' out to the four pubs once a week.

An alternative to the Partner Service is a 'Hosted Service'. This entails a sub-postmaster (or one of their staff) visiting a locality on a regular basis to open a post office for a limited number of hours. Such post offices are typically found in village or church halls – the very essence of a community post office. The Cathedral and Church Buildings Division of the Church of England, the Methodist Church and the United Reformed Church have sought opportunities for church buildings to host 'outreach' post offices in order to preserve postal services, particularly in rural communities.

A 'Home Service' also enables customers to order products and services by telephone. A post office then arranges for them to be delivered to their home. This service has appealed more to isolated businesses than individuals.

In 2000 sub-postmasters ran 97 per cent of post offices, accounting for 80 per cent of Post Office turnover. These post offices, frequently in rural locations, were very important to local communities. Such offices, particularly when situated in the local village shop, remained an important meeting point for local residents. However, difficulties can arise when a sub-postmaster retires or dies. Around 10 per cent of post offices change hands each year and it can be difficult to find a suitable location for a replacement in what are often described as 'amenity deprived areas'. Many rural sub-postmasters see running a post office as 'a way of life' rather than as a means to make money. It is not often that an individual would run a post office as an investment, though many sub-postmasters sell their business on retirement as a means of supplementing their pension.

In the belief that there was an over-provision of post offices in urban areas, the decision was made in 1984 to close a number of sub-post offices where the sub-postmaster was willing to volunteer for redundancy. 535 post offices were proposed for closure, of which 261 were closed during that year. Hundreds more followed soon after. Many crown post offices were also closed or reduced to sub-post office status. Another plan was implemented in 1989 – to convert 250 crown post offices to agency offices staffed by Post Office Counters employees, enabling a further reduction in costs to the business.

Kim Charles, sub-postmistress at Scole, Norfolk, just before her post office closed in October 2008.

Wendy Batten, postmistress at Ulpha post office and general store near Broughton-in-Furness, Cumbria, had to purchase a new post office sign at her own expense when a delivery lorry knocked off the old one. Holidaymakers supplement the trade generated from the scattered rural community.

An 'Essentials' post office in the Premier store, Old Town, Hastings, Sussex. 'Essentials' post offices appeared in 2009.

As part of a 'Network Change' programme, the Post Office closed some 2,500 post offices up to 2007, leaving around 14,300 post offices in the United Kingdom. Post offices had been closed in the past but this had invariably been voluntary on the part of the sub-postmaster and had occasionally left gaps in the network. This dramatic and wide-ranging sweep of new closures was very different. The Post Office now had the power to close post offices compulsorily. Needless to say, many of the closures were unpopular and considerable numbers of often heated public hearings were held. Forty-two public consultations led to just ninety-two offices being saved from closure. The intention was that some five hundred of the closed offices would be replaced by the new outreach facilities such as churches, public houses and village halls. These were a tried and tested formula, as demonstrated by 150 community-owned shops across the United Kingdom, many of which incorporated a post office.

The government's range of proposed measures was intended to modernise and reshape the post office network and put it on a stable footing. Though recognising that 'Post offices play an important social and economic role in the communities they serve', a 2006 report by the Department of Trade and Industry highlighted that 'with new technology, changing lifestyles and a wider choice of accessing services, people are visiting post offices less', rendering the network 'unsustainable in its present form'.

The post office inside Sainsbury's Savacentre at Merton in south-west London opened in 1990 – the first to be run under a franchise agreement.

A further response was a commercial deal with retailer W. H. Smith, starting in 2006 with a trial of six crown post offices being franchised to W. H. Smith's shops. These were in Altrincham, Ashton-under-Lyne, Hammersmith, Shrewsbury, Slough and Swansea. Pronounced a success, post office relocation to W. H. Smith has grown since 2007. These new-style crown offices feature 'open plan' counters. Cash drawers are shared between counter staff, enabling the post offices to hold far less money than previously, reducing security risks. When Postwatch paid a visit to the franchised post

Impression from a self-inking date-stamp used at an 'Essentials' post office.

Himish (Harry) Amin, sub-postmaster at the Old Town Stores and Essentials post office, Hastings. He provides about 85 per cent of the services that the Post Office offers, including pensions, parcels and post. The office is open the same hours as the shop – 7 a.m. to 10 p.m., even on Sundays.

From August 2007 seventy crown post offices were relocated in branches of the retailer W. H. Smith. Their open-plan design resembled that of high street banks and building societies.

office at Hammersmith, it pronounced it 'a pragmatic solution to ensuring the continuation of access to postal and Post Office services for customers at a reduced cost but with no apparent reduction in service'.

Modern post offices have to keep pace with external innovation and customer expectations if they are to survive. Post offices may have grown up around social mail but the type of customer has changed over the centuries. The general public appreciate the service, friendly greeting and individual concern that they receive in their local post office but in the twenty-first century business customers account for 90 per cent of the mail. Such customers expect far more from their local post office. They want tracking of mail and competitive prices; an international end-to-end service is expected. The gulf between those responsible for enabling a profitable business and those most vulnerable or in need of a social service has never been so wide.

A touch-screen 'Post & Go' postage label vending machine in use at Maidstone post office, Kent. These particular machines were part of a limited trial that took place in 2007 prior to the introduction of similar machines in seven hundred offices throughout Britain from October 2008.

Since 2000, modern sub-offices have fallen into five contract types, outlined in *Counter Revolution: Modernising the Post Office Network* (a PIU report, June 2000):

Scale-payment (14,900 outlets): fixed payment element specific to each post office. Contract based on three months notice on either side.

Community (2,000 outlets): similar to scale-payment contract, but fixed payment partly dependent on opening hours.

Modified (660 outlets): the contract for branch conversions; similar to a scale-payment contract but offices have a £15,000 fixed payment element.

Company franchise (225 outlets): five-year franchise agreement aimed at multiple retailers who require higher standards for capital investment and service levels. Payments made up of a variable element plus a volume-related premium.

Independent franchise (45 outlets): similar to a company franchise contract but aimed at non-multiple retailers.

The modern post office on Camden High Street in north London provides a wide range of services. When photographed in 2009, it provided a ticketing system to direct customers to the appropriate counter. 'Post & Go' vending machines were also installed. The office is occasionally used to trial new products.

New post offices are now equipped with level access or ramped approaches. Many existing offices have also been adapted and low-level writing facilities are provided for customers using wheelchairs.

In May 2007 the Government set out the minimum access criteria intended to maintain a national network of post offices and protect vulnerable customers in deprived urban, rural and remote areas:

- Nationally, 99 per cent of the UK population to be within 3 miles and 90 per cent of the population to be within 1 mile of their nearest post office outlet.

- 99 per cent of the total population in deprived urban areas across the UK to be within 1 mile of their nearest post office outlet.

- 95 per cent of the total urban population across the UK to be within 1 mile of their nearest post office outlet.

- 95 per cent of the total rural population across the UK to be within 3 miles of their nearest post office outlet.

In addition, for each individual postcode district:

- 95 per cent of the population of the postcode district to be within 6 miles of their nearest post office counter.

Haroldswick, Shetland, Scotland

Painswick, Gloucestershire, England

Beddgelert, Gwynedd, Cymru/Wales

Ballyroney, County Down, Northern Ireland

In 1997 a stamp issue commemorated the centenary of the National Federation of Sub-Postmasters. Post offices in Scotland, England, Wales and Northern Ireland were depicted: 20p, Haroldswick, Shetland; 26p, Painswick, Gloucestershire; 43p, Beddgelert, Gwynedd; 63p, Ballyroney, County Down.

Sanquhar post office, Dumfries and Galloway, is probably the oldest post office in the United Kingdom, and possibly the world. There is evidence of an office at this location as long ago as 1763.

When the Rural Development Commission carried out a survey of rural services in each parish in England in 1997 it concluded that only public houses had greater coverage than post offices. It is small wonder that a post office can act as the centre for information within a community – news of engagements, marriages, births and deaths, accidents and illness, examination results and village fetes – as well as providing items for sale. Information and gossip is as much sought at the post office counter as a stamp. Despite changes in national economies, world wars, strikes and competition, thousands of local post offices continue to thrive, offering products and services to meet a range of needs. Though the structural format of post offices may change and their services adapt, they are likely to remain a feature of our cities, towns and villages for some time to come.

FURTHER READING

Apart from a number of specific articles and media reports, there has been surprisingly little written on post offices. The subject is touched upon in the following publications:

Austin, Brian. *English Provincial Posts 1633–1840*. Phillimore, 1978.

Clarke, Jonathan. *Purpose Built Post Offices: A Desk-Based Assessment of Building Type*. English Heritage, 2008.

Daunton, Martin. *Royal Mail: The Post Office since 1840*. Athlone Press, 1985.

Department of Trade and Industry. *The Post Office Network: Government Response to Public Consultation*. May 2007.

Donald, Archie. *The Posts of Sevenoaks in Kent*. Woodvale Press, 1992.

Farrugia, Jean Young. *The Letter Box*. Centaur Press, 1969.

Johannessen, Neil. *Telephone Boxes*. Shire, 1994.

Joyce, Herbert. *The History of the Post Office from Its Establishment Down to 1836*. London, 1893.

Osley, Julian. *Post Office Architecture*. The British Postal Museum & Archive, 2010.

Rennie, Paul. *Design: GPO Posters*. Antique Collectors' Club, 2010.

Robinson, Howard. *Britain's Post Office*. Oxford University Press, 1953.

Robinson, Martin. *Old Letter Boxes*. Shire, 2000.

Stray, Julian. *Moving the Mail ... by Road*. The British Postal Museum & Archive, 2006.

Wilkinson, Frederick. *Royal Mail Coaches: An Illustrated History*. Tempus Publishing, 2007.

PLACES TO VISIT

The British Postal Museum & Archive is the leading resource for British postal heritage. It cares for the visual, physical and written records of over four hundred years of postal heritage, including stamps, poster design, photography, staff records and vehicles. It is custodian of two significant collections: the Royal Mail Archive, and the museum collection of the former National Postal Museum. The Royal Mail Archive is designated as being of outstanding national importance. To find out more, visit: www.postalheritage.org.uk

The British Postal Museum & Archive, Freeling House, Phoenix Place, London WC1X 0DL. Telephone: 020 7239 2570. Website: www.postalheritage.org.uk Public search room for archive items including Post Office records, photographs and stamp artwork, based in Central London, open throughout the week. Museum store in Debden, Essex, containing larger items including pillar boxes and vehicles, open on selected dates throughout the year.

The British Postal Museum & Archive Museum of the Post Office in the Community and replica Victorian post office, Blists Hill Victorian Village, Ironbridge Gorge Museums, Coalbrookdale, Telford, Shropshire TF8 7DQ. Website www.ironbridge.org.uk

A mobile post office was introduced in October 1936 for use at county shows, race meetings and other events. It was an immediate success. This is the cover to a booklet produced to explain the services provided.

INDEX

Page numbers in italics refer to illustrations